THE ULTIMATE

RHINE RIVER

CRUISE TRAVEL

GUIDE

A Comprehensive Guide to Experiencing the Best
of Culture, Cuisine, and Adventure Along the
Rhine River Cruise Route.

By

STERLING BLANTON

Contents

CHAPTER ONE

CRUISING THE RHINE RIVER

One of the world's most well-known and stunning waterways for cruising is the Rhine River. It travels from its source in Switzerland to the Netherlands via Germany's scenic heartland, passing through Alpine Mountain ranges, winding Riesling vineyards, Heidi-style valleys, and renowned towns and cities before emptying into the North Sea. Basel, Cologne, Frankfurt, the Rhine Valley, a UNESCOs World Heritage Site dotted with abandoned and rebuilt hilltop castles and villages, as well as the Dutch city of Amsterdam, are major Rhine cities. Cologne is known for its Gothic cathedral. The Rhine is a fascinating and thrilling river to cruise on, with so many various routes and ports of stop available. It is the second-longest river in Western Europe after the Danube.

The Rhine River, sometimes referred to as the River Rhine, is an 800-mile-long European river that is home to a diverse array of landscapes, cuisine, wine, and cultural traditions. Rhine River cruise is a convenient and comfortable method to see the continent because it passes through six nations: Switzerland, Liechtenstein, Austria, Germany, France, and the Netherlands.

There are certain simple but crucial details you should be aware of before making a reservation for a river cruise on the Rhine. In order to help you prepare and have a better idea of what to expect, we've provided a brief summary of Rhine River information below.

Where Is the Rhine River?

The Rhine River flows through Europe, starting as a trickle of melted snow from the Rheinwaldhorn Glacier in the Swiss Alps and ending at Rotterdam, where it merges into the North Sea. It is 800 kilometers long and traverses six different European nations, as was already noted.

There are numerous European rivers that the Rhine River intersects with. The Moselle River, which flows beyond Luxembourg into France to the southwest, the Neckar, which flows southeast from Mannheim to Heidelberg, and the Main, which flows southeast from Mainz through to Frankfurt, are just a few of the numerous tributaries of the Rhine.

A network of canals connects the River Rhine to other significant European rivers, such as the Seine, Elbe, Rhone, and Saone. One significant canal is the

Rhine-Main-Danube Canal, which begins east of Frankfurt and connects the Rhine with the Danube.

The Rhine River's Castles and Other Stunning Views

Get ready to explore the meandering lanes of peaceful medieval villages, visit ancient castles and verdant vineyards, savor the charm of historic cities like Mainz and Strasbourg, and take in the energy of pulsating contemporary cities like Cologne and Basel.

Be warned that fantasy castles do not line the entire Rhine. The majority are concentrated along the Upper Middle Rhine River, which runs between the German towns of Koblenz and Rudesheim. This river is famous for its stunning Rhine Gorge, which is placed on the UNESCO World Heritage List. Along the Rhine, there are many places to admire and fall in love.

Despite the Rhine's importance, not all of its natural beauty is appealing. Much of it is, but you must also account for the sporadic sighting of a factory or power plant, especially in and near more industrialized areas like the Basel outskirts.

Why choose the Rhine

The Rhine is the second-longest river in Central and Western Europe, and as such, it provides an abundance of diverse itineraries and cruises. Cruise lines offer itineraries ranging from a few days to two weeks, giving you the option of taking long, peaceful vacations or short, enjoyable Rhine river cruises. Passing through Switzerland, Germany, and the Netherlands allows cruisers to explore many countries. A-Rosa, CroisiEurope, and Fred Olsen River vacations are some of the more affordable cruise companies that sail the Rhine, while Viking, Tauck, and AmaWaterways are more expensive lines that provide luxurious rhine vacations. Scenic and Uniworld, two luxury cruise lines, also travel this remarkable canal. You'll have a great time cruising down this tranquil canal, whether you choose an overnight Rhine River cruise or one of the top day cruises.

Why go on a Cruise on the Rhine?

There is no single explanation that can explain why the Rhine River is so popular as a destination for cruises. Instead, it is a confluence of elements, each of which adds to the waterway's allure.

- Numerous Itineraries

The Rhine River is a master of adaptability, providing a variety of routes to suit various interests and time constraints. You can select a cruise schedule that meets your needs whether you have a week or just a few days to spare. Shorter excursions give a delicious taste of the

Rhine charm, while longer cruises enable you to fully immerse yourself in the area, discovering its undiscovered gems and well-known features.

- Cruising Lines at All Price Points

The Rhine accommodates a wide range of tourists, from those looking for affordable options to those seeking the height of luxury. A-Rosa, CroisiEurope, and Fred Olsen River Cruises are some of the most budget-friendly cruise companies that sail the Rhine. These lines make sure that tourists on a budget can still enjoy the Rhine's magnificence.

Viking, Tauck, and AmaWaterways are at the top end of the market and provide a degree of sophistication and quality that raises the cruise experience to new heights. The extravagant offerings of Scenic and Uniworld offer an unsurpassed level of luxury and enjoyment. Travelers from various walks of life can choose the ideal cruise line for their itinerary thanks to the range of cruise lines.

- A rich cultural history

With cities, towns, and villages lining its banks that have witnessed centuries of European legacy, the Rhine River is a passageway of culture and history. The Rhine offers treasures waiting to be found at every port of call, whether you are an obsessive history buff, an architecture aficionado, or just a tourist with a curious spirit.

- Natural Beauty

The stunning scenery along the Rhine will comfort nature lovers and enthusiasts. You go along the river through stunning Alpine landscapes, lush vineyards, and tranquil valleys. It is a journey through constantly-changing landscapes that amazes and surprises travelers, providing moments of breathtaking beauty.

- A sense of Adventure

The Rhine River cruise experience goes beyond the ship for people who enjoy adventure. Opportunities for active exploration and discovery include excursions into the nearby countryside, riding along riverbank walks, and exploring the cobblestone alleyways of old towns.

CHAPTER TWO

The Rhine River Route

- A Swiss Alpine

Your trip along the Rhine begins high in the Swiss Alps, the river's humble birthplace. The Rhine emerges from the Lai da Tuma, a tiny glacial lake, hidden within the mountains, as a pure, clear torrent. A thrilling journey is put in motion as the river acquires momentum and grows in strength as it flows from the alpine heights.

- Switzerland, Basel

Basel, the political, social, and economic center of Switzerland, is the first key stop along the Rhine River route. You are welcomed by Basel's fusion of heritage and modernity. Explore the city's quaint old town, or Altstadt, whose streets lead to ancient structures, churches, and bustling market squares.

One of Europe's oldest art museums, the Kunstmuseum Basel, exhibits a staggering variety of pieces from numerous historical periods.

- The Rhine Valley of Germany

The Rhine's majestic beauty is fully appreciated as it flows into Germany's heartland as it moves north. The Rhine River has had a lasting impact on the history and culture of Europe, as seen by the Rhine Valley, which is a UNESCO World Heritage Site.

- France's Strasbourg

The Rhine briefly meanders through Strasbourg, a city with a distinctive fusion of French and German elements, just before it enters Germany. A marvel of Gothic architecture, the Strasbourg Cathedral dominates the skyline and provides breathtaking 360-degree views from its tower. Discover the charming La Petite France neighborhood, famous for its winding canals and half-timbered homes.

- Speyer

In Speyer, one of Germany's oldest cities, you arrive after continuing along the Rhine River route. Visit the Speyer Cathedral, a masterpiece of Romanesque architecture and a UNESCO World Heritage Site, here. The charming Altportel (Old Gate) offers charming views of the city, while the Historical Museum of the Palatinate offers insights into the history of the region.

- Heidelberg

As you continue traveling, you reach Heidelberg, a city renowned for its allure and home to the recognizable Heidelberg Castle. The castle, which is perched on a hill above the city, is a representation of both medieval and Renaissance design. Take in the breathtaking views of the city and the Neckar River as you stroll along the Philosopher's Walk.

- Rhine Gorge: Legends and Castles

The Rhine enters the enthralling Rhine Gorge as it continues to flow, a section known for its stunning vistas, vineyard-covered slopes, and an almost infinite number of castles set on steep cliffs. This is the land of fables and legends.

- Loreley Rock and Rüdesheim

With its cobblestone alleys and vineyards, the picturesque wine town of Rüdesheim entices visitors. For sweeping views of the Rhine Valley, take a trip on the Rhine cable car. With legends of seductive sirens tempting sailors to their doom, the Loreley Rock sits as a mythological protector of the river further downstream.

- Koblenz

Koblenz is a historical city located where the Moselle and Rhine rivers converge. Where the two rivers meet, a well-known landmark is called the Deutsches Eck. Visit the Ehrenbreitstein Fortress, which offers commanding views of the confluence, and explore the ancient old town.

- Cologne

A highlight of each Rhine River trip is Cologne, home to the magnificent Kölner Dom. One of Europe's most recognizable sights and a UNESCO World Heritage Site is this Gothic masterpiece. Discover the crowded downtown streets, indulge in a Kölsch beer, and take in the lively ambiance along the Rhine promenade.

- Rotterdam and Amsterdam are in the Dutch Lowlands.

As the Rhine approaches its terminus, it passes through the Netherlands' flatlands, providing a stark contrast to the gorge's stunning beauty.

- Rotterdam

Modern metropolis Rotterdam is home to cutting-edge architecture and a strong arts community. For a flavor of the city's avant-garde character, visit the Cube Houses, the Erasmus Bridge, and the Museum Boijmans Van Beuningen.

- Amsterdam

Your trip down the Rhine River path comes to an end in the charming Dutch capital city of Amsterdam. Visit renowned institutions like the Rijksmuseum and the Van Gogh Museum, explore the city's gorgeous canals, and take in the bustling street life. An Amsterdam canal tour is the ideal way to cap off your Rhine vacation.

- THE BEST TIME TO GO

- The weather is often sunny and warm from mid-June through August during the height of summer. However, with so many cruise ships cruising the Rhine, there are more people (cruisers and other tourists) at famous tourist locations. Low water levels are also more likely to occur in the summer, which can be very disruptive and force last-minute itinerary adjustments, missed excursions, and extended bus rides when the river is impassable. Additionally, prices are typically highest during this period.

- When the weather is more moderate, there are less crowds, and rates are a little bit lower, more tourists are choosing to sail in the shoulder seasons of spring (late April to May) and fall (September to mid-October). The best deals on cruises can be found during off-peak seasons (early to mid-April and mid-October through November), but keep in mind that it can get chilly and wet. The Rhine Gorge and other Rhine parts are especially stunning in the fall when the foliage change to vivid red, golden, and yellow hues.

- Easter is another great time to take a Rhine cruise since local markets are filled with colorfully painted eggs, gorgeous wooden ornaments, and lovely flowers.

Also think about scheduling a Rhine cruise for one of the region's breathtaking "Rhine in Flames" summer and fall festivals. These take place at various locations along the Middle Rhine and feature spectacular fireworks displays as well as festivals of music and dancing. They are typically associated with local wine festivals or other celebrations.

Another popular time to travel is from late November to mid-December because the Rhine Christmas markets and holiday decorations create a lovely ambience.

What to pack and clothing pack for a Rhine River cruise

Packing for a River Rhine cruise is an essential part of ensuring a comfortable and memorable journey. The key is to strike a balance between practicality, comfort, and style, taking into account the changing weather and the range of activities you may engage in. Here's a comprehensive packing list to help you prepare for your River Rhine adventure:

1. Clothing:

- **Layered Clothing:** Given the variable weather, pack a mix of lightweight, breathable layers. Include short-sleeve shirts, long-sleeve shirts, sweaters, and a lightweight jacket or windbreaker.

- **Comfortable Walking Shoes:** Opt for comfortable, supportive walking shoes for excursions and exploration.

- **Dressy Outfits:** Depending on your cruise line and personal preferences, you may want a few dressier outfits for evening dinners or special events.

- **Rain Gear:** A compact umbrella and a waterproof jacket can be a lifesaver in case of unexpected rain.

- **Swimwear:** If your cruise ship has a pool or hot tub, bring swimwear.

2. Accessories:

- **Hat:** A wide-brimmed hat for sun protection or a warm beanie for chilly days.

- **Sunglasses:** Quality sunglasses with UV protection are essential.

- **Scarves and Gloves:** For cooler days, especially if you plan on being outside.

- **Convertible Day Bag:** A lightweight, foldable day bag for carrying essentials during shore excursions.

3. Toiletries:

- **Travel-sized Toiletries:** Shampoo, conditioner, soap, toothpaste, and any other personal items you need. Many cruises provide basic toiletries, but it's always good to have your favorites.

- **Prescription Medications:** Ensure you have an adequate supply for the duration of your cruise.

- **Sunscreen:** Especially important if you plan to spend time on the ship's deck.

- **Insect Repellent:** Depending on the season and itinerary, this may come in handy for excursions.

- **First Aid Kit:** A basic kit with band-aids, pain relievers, and any necessary medications.

4. Electronics:

- **Camera or Smartphone:** Capture the stunning landscapes and memorable moments along the Rhine.

- **Adapters and Chargers:** European-style power adapters and chargers for your devices.

- **Portable Charger:** Handy for keeping your devices charged while on excursions.

5. Travel Documents:

- **Passport and Visa:** Ensure your passport is valid for at least six months beyond your travel dates and that you have any necessary visas.

- **Cruise Documents:** Keep copies of your cruise booking confirmations and travel insurance information.

- **Credit Cards and Cash:** Notify your bank of your travel plans and carry some local currency for small expenses.

6. Entertainment and Reading Material:

- **Books, E-Reader, or Magazines:** Enjoy some reading during leisurely moments on the ship.

- **Travel Guide:** A guidebook or digital app with information about the Rhine's ports of call can enhance your experience.

7. Miscellaneous Items:

- **Reusable Water Bottle:** Staying hydrated is essential, and many ships have water stations for refilling.

- **Travel Pillow and Eye Mask:** For more comfortable sleep during your journey.

- **Laundry Bag:** To keep your dirty clothes separate from clean ones.

- **Ziplock Bags:** Useful for storing snacks, organizing small items, or keeping things dry.

- **Travel Wallet or Money Belt:** A secure way to carry important documents and valuables.

- **Language Phrasebook:** If you're interested in local languages, a small phrasebook can be helpful and appreciated by locals.

8. Optional Items:

- **Binoculars:** Enhance your views of the stunning scenery.

- **Reusable Shopping Bag:** Useful for carrying souvenirs or groceries in port towns.

- **Travel Journal:** Document your experiences and memories.

For your cruise, you can bring only carryon luggage. You can bring only carryon luggage. If you have limited mobility, remember to carry a pair of comfortable shoes for walking ashore and to be aware that many river stops require climbing at least a few steps.

The weather might be unpredictable even in the summer, so carry a raincoat or weatherproof parka. A fleece blanket and a scarf are also suggested as additional layers.

Even though river cruise attire is typically quite informal, you should pack something finer for dinner, especially if you're fortunate enough to be invited to the Captain's Table. A shawl or pashmina can also keep you warm on chilly dining room nights or windy sailing days outside on deck.

If you have trouble falling asleep and don't want to be startled awake by early morning rumblings when your boat departs from its overnight stop and travels through locks, bring earplugs.

Binoculars may be provided in each cabin on some river liners, but make sure before you travel. They're fantastic for getting up-close views of life along the riverbanks and for getting a clear perspective of landmarks like the Rhine Gorge's Lorelei statue and castles perched on cliffs. If your ship does not have US two-pin plugs, pack an adaptor to accommodate your phone or other gadgets.

CHAPTER THREE

THE TOP DESTINATIONS FOR A RHINE RIVER CRUISE

The Rhine River is one of the longest in Europe, and its banks are home to many amazing places. Along its 820-mile course through the Netherlands, France, Germany, and Switzerland, the Rhine passes a variety of locations, including clifftop castles in the Upper Middle Rhine Valley and Amsterdam's canals.

Look no further than the Rhine if scenery, history, cuisine, or wine are on your list of must-see attractions. And whether you choose a brief Christmas market cruise or a one- or two-week tour, there's a good chance you'll experience some of the trendiest locations along the Rhine River.

Check out some of the top Rhine River cruise destinations and some lesser-known gems you may stop at along the route to help you plan your boat vacation.

Germany's Upper Middle Rhine Valley:

When you approach the Upper Middle Rhine Valley, the most scenic location along the Rhine River, you'll want to be outside on the deck. More than 40 castles and fortifications border the banks of the 40-mile river between Bingen and Koblenz in Germany, which is a UNESCO World Heritage site.

Fear not, if history isn't precisely your thing; this is also an oenophile's paradise. Germany's most well-known wine-growing region is bounded by the luxuriant vineyards of the Upper Middle Rhine Valley.

Inspirational Cityscapes & Van Gogh Paintings in Amsterdam

Amsterdam is an excellent Rhine River location because of its recognizable canals. A Rhine River cruise is frequently started or ended in Amsterdam. Ships land directly in the center of the vibrant and culturally diverse Dutch city, which, according to estimates, is home to over 800,000 bicycles. Amsterdam is a labyrinth of canals that is ideal for exploring on foot (or by bike, assuming you can handle the two-wheel traffic).

The most well-known destination in the area is the Anne Frank House, which features moving displays like the Jewish schoolgirl's diary from the Second World War. You should also visit the Van Gogh Museum and the Rijksmuseum to admire Dutch treasures like Rembrandt's "The Night Watch."

Amsterdam's many springtime Rhine cruises include bulb sailings by vast fields of tulips, which further add to the splendor of this location.

Beautiful Cathedral and Iconic Local Beer in Cologne, Germany

Cologne, Germany, is one of the most well-known Rhine River locations. You can't get lost in the city because of the 515-foot spires of the UNESCO-listed cathedral, which dominate the skyline and can be seen from every cruise ship landing location. The Cologne Cathedral was constructed over the course of more than 600 years, and the expansive views from the top of the south spire make the 509-step ascent worthwhile. Afterward, relax with a locally produced beer at one of the Rhine's riverfront bars; kolsch beers, which are typically harsh and hop-forward, are popular in the Cologne area. Visit the Cologne Chocolate Museum if that is still insufficient.

Charming Streetscapes and Alsatian Culture in Strasbourg, France

Strasbourg, the fascinating city of France's Alsace region, which borders Germany and Switzerland and has been molded over time by various cultures, is a popular stop on Rhine River cruises. Strasbourg, the smallest region in France, has been referred to as the capital of Europe because it is home to the European Parliament and other significant E.U. institutions. Highlights of Strasbourg include the picturesque Petite France neighborhood, where canals are bordered by half-timbered buildings, and the lopsided one-towered church with a spectacular astronomical clock with animated figures.

The Netherlands' Kinderdijk: Iconic Dutch Vistas

The largest concentration of antique windmills in the Netherlands may be found in Kinderdijk, one of the top Rhine River locations to complete your travel photography. 19 windmills can be seen up close here, and you can even go inside several of them. You can also watch a movie and see how the Dutch manage to survive on land that is below sea level. You can purchase a pair of wooden clogs, another well-known Dutch icon, in the gift shop near the entrance.

Heidelberg, Germany: A Historical Castle and Academic Candy

Mark Twain, an American author, once stated about Heidelberg, Germany, "I have never enjoyed a view which had such a satisfying charm about it as this one gives." And the location continues to enchant Rhine River boaters with its rich history and quaint cityscapes. Since it was struck in both 1537 and 1764, the Heidelberg Castle, a commanding landmark over the city, disproves the myth that lightning never strikes twice. Heidelberg institution, Germany's oldest institution, is located in Heidelberg, which is also well-known for its studentenkuss, or "student kiss," which are sweets that were first produced in the 19th century and are excellent keepsakes. In the heart of the city, try them at Cafe Knosel.

Germany's Breisach: Fairy Tales and Famous Cake

Breisach serves as the entry point to Germany's dense and mountainous Black Forest, the legendary location for the Grimm Brothers' fairy tale "Hansel and Gretel." In this Rhine River destination, typical shore excursions are equally fantastic. You could also stop by a workshop that makes cuckoo clocks and sample real Black Forest cake (schwarzwalder kirschtorte).

Other trips are more solemn, such as excursions to sad World War II locations in the Colmar Pocket, one of the final areas of France that German forces held control of. Legendary battles here include the one in which 19-year-old American soldier-turned-actor Audie Murphy defeated an entire German platoon by himself.

Wine, music boxes, and a scenic cable car ride in Rudesheim, Germany

Rudesheim, a charming German winemaking village, is one of the more intimate Rhine River cruise stops. You can walk or take a land rail to the busy Drosselgasse street, where quaint pubs serve regional riesling and brandy-and-cream-infused Rudesheimer coffee. Siegfried's Mechanical Music Cabinet Museum, where the exhibits vary from tiny music boxes to carnival organs, is one of the more eccentric local Rudesheim attractions. Take a beautiful cable car journey above the vineyards to the striking Niederwald monument overlooking the Rhine to cap off your day.

Basel, Switzerland

Start or end your cruise in Basel, Switzerland's cultural hub. Explore the historic old town, museums, and the scenic beauty of the Rhine in this vibrant city.

Rotterdam, Netherlands

A modern metropolis with innovative architecture and a thriving cultural scene. Visit the Cube Houses, Erasmus Bridge, and the Museum Boijmans Van Beuningen.

Swiss Alps, Switzerland

While not a city or town, the Swiss Alps offer breathtaking scenery and the source of the Rhine River. Consider adding a pre-cruise excursion to explore the Alpine landscapes.

Mainz, Germany

Known for its historic old town, Mainz is a city steeped in history and culture. Visit the Mainz Cathedral and the Gutenberg Museum.

Take note, history buffs and museum visitors—this one's for you! German city of Mainz has a number of art and history museums that are sure to keep you occupied throughout this stop. It is close to the Main River and on the Rhine's banks. The Romans founded the city of Mainz in the first century, making it a very historic city. The Gutenberg, which honors the creator of the metal type printing method, which revolutionized business throughout the industrial revolution, is one of the most well-known museums.

These are just a few of the top destinations you can explore on a River Rhine cruise. Each offers a unique blend of history, culture, and natural beauty, making your journey along the Rhine a truly memorable experience.

Neuschwanstein Castle:

A very well-liked tourist destination in Germany's Bavaria region is this fairytale castle. It's likely that excursions to Neuschwanstein will be offered if your Rhine River cruise stops in Munich. The Black Forest-based Neuschwanstein castle, which conjures up images of princesses and fairy tales, served as one of the models for Walt Disney's Sleeping Beauty castle.

German Heidelberg Castle:

The Rhine River passes through Germany in large portions, thus many traditional and picturesque German towns will be on your itinerary. Heidelberg is a wonderful location for those who enjoy architecture and displays traditional German charm. The "Old Bridge" in the city, which spans the river in the direction of Heidelberg Castle and makes for a fantastic photo opportunity, is famous.

French village of Strasbourg

This is the place to go if you're seeking for a traditional European country town. Strasbourg has a distinctly French vibe thanks to its cobblestoned streets, boutiques, and cathedral, of course. If you want to follow in Marie Antoinette's footsteps, make sure to go to the charming Petite France, the town's historic district, and Rohan Palace. Strasbourg is a lovely location to go to for Christmas markets.

Palatinate Forest Rhine River cruise views of the forest

This vast tract of lush forest in Germany could only conceal castles and animals from fairy tales. A highlight of any journey down the Rhine is seeing the forest rise up on the banks from the viewing deck of your river cruise. Though several hiking and biking trails wind through the forest, not all Rhine River cruises will make a stop to take advantage of this opportunity.

Koblenz, Along the Rhine River, Koblenz

At the meeting point of the Rhine and Moselle rivers, Koblenz, one of Germany's oldest cities, serves as the entrance to the Rhine Gorge. The city of Koblenz is well-known for its historic structures, wine sampling, gardens, and quirky art installations and museums.

Cologne

Cologne is one of the most well-known tourist locations in Germany, not least because of its magnificent Cathedral. It is a standard stop on any Rhine River cruise. The city of Cologne, a significant trading hub for many centuries, is a sight to behold. Tourists frequently visit art museums, but if you'd rather avoid being inside, you may simply stroll along the charming alleys along the river for breathtaking vistas and people watching.

Lucerne

Wandering the streets of this lovely city is one of the greatest ways to experience it. Your stroll will take you through charming cafes, lovely bridges, and candy stores filled with a variety of delicacies for chocolate lovers. If you prefer being outside, schedule a ride on Lake Lucerne and spend some time discovering its features.

Zurich

Zurich successfully blends modern trade with pre-medieval culture. The capital is a financial and banking hub, making it a major international economic hub. Zurich is known as the capital of the banking industry and offers several excellent shopping options. If you like being outside, take a train from the city's main railway station to one of the neighboring high summits. At the top of the Uetliberg, hikers may take in a 360-degree view of Zurich. Later, you can visit the nearby spectacular rivers and lakes, which are also great for swimming.

Rüdesheim

You can select between taking a gondola ride, trekking through vineyards, or visiting Siegfried's Mechanical Musical Instrument Museum when you stop in Rüdesheim.

Because it allows you to sample their world-famous Riesling wine, hiking through the vineyards is a popular pastime in the city. Visitors can learn about the history of their well-known wines while they observe the winemaking process. While visiting Rüdesheim, you should explore the medieval-style castles with cobblestone streets that are located near the vineyard. Later, you can take a cable car up to the Niederwald monument above the vineyards, where you can shop before returning to the cruise ship.

Castles from fairy tales on the Rhine

- <u>Benrath Palace</u>

In the heart of Puerto del Rossario, there is a charming church.This elegant structure was constructed in 1756 as a "maison de plaisance," or pleasure palace. After seeing the sculptures and pieces of art from the 18th century in its two museums, take a stroll through the lovely gardens, which are home to more than 80 different bird species.

- <u>Eltz Castle</u>

In the heart of Puerto del Rossario, there is a charming church.

The historic Eltz Castle, regarded as one of Germany's most charming castles, is located in the heart of the picturesque Eltz Forest nature reserve.

Since 1157, the same family has owned the castle. Several of its hundred rooms, notably the Armory and the intriguing Rodendorf kitchen from the fifteenth century, are open for tours today.

- The Reichsburg Castle

In the heart of Puerto del Rossario, there is a charming church.The castle, also known as Burg Cochem, rises nearly 300 feet above the river and commands the entire skyline.

Over 90% of this castle was faithfully rebuilt on the original site, despite having a history dating back to the 11th century. The largest of the Neo-Gothic halls, the Rittersaal (or Knights' Hall), has a number of hidden corridors filled with period-appropriate furniture and armor. Women accused of witchcraft are purportedly thrown from the topmost window of the Hexenturn, also known as the "Witches Tower."

- The Castle at Rudesheim

Rudesheim is a lovely village situated at a bend in the Rhine in the center of Germany and is a traditional Christmas cruise stop. It's a terrific location for exploring on foot, indulging in regional fare, shopping, trying wine, and seeing castles. A "Rudesheimer coffee" is one of the delicacies you should try. This delightful alcoholic mixture is presented in a particular kind of cup and is made with whipped cream and flambe brandy. It was created in 1957 and is well-liked by both residents and visitors.

- Cochem

In the heart of Puerto del Rossario, there is a charming church. As you make your way up from the river, the cobblestone streets of Cochem's "Altstadt," or Old Town, will transport you back in time. Take in the gabled, half-timbered homes and the 1739 baroque Rathaus (Town Hall), which is located in the market square.

- Heidelberg

Enjoy breathtaking views of Heidelberg, the river, and the Neckar valley by taking the funicular up to the iconic Heidelberg Castle from the Kornmarkt (town center).

Later, cross the recognizable Old Bridge to take a stroll along Philosopher's Walk, where university professors congregate to take in the breathtaking view of the town and castle across the river.

Brömserburg Castle is a must-see for wine enthusiasts. A remarkable wine museum with more than 2,000 exhibits is housed in one of the Middle Rhine's oldest castles.

- Strasbourg

Fuerteventura is a haven for aloe vera. This multiracial superpower blends medieval allure with political heft from Europe. Explore the historic structures that line the canals at the Grande Île, a UNESCO World Heritage site, to begin your journey. One of the world's highest churches, the Cathédrale Notre Dame de Strasbourg was built in the early 11th century. The fascinating astronomical clock and the lovely stained-glass windows from the 12th century are of great appeal. Go to the Quartier des Tanneurs, which is located at the westernmost point of the Grande Île. Every step is an opportunity for a photo, and there are a ton of cute little cafes serving food and drinks.

- The Rock of Lorelei

The fabled girl who, in despair over an unfaithful lover, threw herself into the Rhine and was changed into a siren who seduced unwary sailors to their doom is the inspiration for the legendary Lorelei Rock near Sankt Goarschausen. The steep, slate rock bearing her name has a statue of her at the top.

CHAPTER FOUR

Honorable Mentions for Rhine River Cruise Locations

Germany's Koblenz: Visit One of the Biggest Castles in Europe

The 19th-century Ehrenbreitstein fortification, one of Europe's largest castles, stands over Koblenz at the meeting point of the Rhine and Moselle. The cable car that crosses the river is the best way to get there. Several fountains that serve as the focal point of the town's squares are just a short stroll from where ships disembark, which is close to the spectacular equestrian statue of Emperor William I.

Historic small town in Cochem, Germany

Some routes depart at Koblenz on the Rhine and go erratically along the Moselle stream before stopping at Cochem. The old town is lined with classic half-timbered black and white homes, and the picture-perfect town is capped by a medieval castle where you can see a huge suit of armor.

Jewish history and remnants of the Roman Empire in Speyer, Germany

Speyer is one of the less visited Rhine River cruise ports. It is one of Germany's oldest towns and an ancient Roman colony known for its substantial Romanesque-style cathedral. A typical mikveh bathhouse from Speyer's rich Jewish heritage dates to 1128.

CHAPTER FIVE

CRUISE LINES AND POPULAR ITINERARIES FOR THE RHINE RIVER

The Rhine River is one of the most sought-after European river cruise itineraries available due to its enormous popularity as a waterway throughout the world. Numerous cruise lines float along its crowded banks as a result of its undeniable popularity among river cruising lovers. From April to October alone, hundreds of riverboats travel down the Rhine, and that doesn't include excursion boats that run short trips along the river for locals to use.

Cruise Lines on the Rhine River Are Numerous and Reliable, they include: Avalon Waterways, AmaWaterways, CroisiEurope, Emerald Cruises, Riviera Travel, Scenic, Uniworld, Vantage Deluxe World Travel, Tauck, and Viking River Cruises are a few of the well-known cruise lines that run on the Rhine River. Itineraries for Rhine River Cruises range in style, duration, and location. There is a Rhine River cruise itinerary to suit every kind of visitor, from quick one-day excursions to in-depth two-week sailings (and more). For Americans, this might include taking a little cruise—four or five nights, for example—in conjunction with a lengthier land-based European holiday.

Three to five-night short river cruises on the Rhine

Sailings on the Rhine River are brief and only last three, four, or five nights. While a five-night journey from medieval Andernach to Cologne via Rüdesheim, Boppard (famous for its Roman fortifications), Koblenz, and Bonn is possible, a usual three-night cruise will sail roundtrip from Strasbourg to Koblenz with an overnight stop at Rüdesheim. This is an excellent way to try river cruising if you've never done it as part of a longer European holiday.

Christmas Market Rhine Cruises

In November and December, when crowds of visitors converge on the Rhine's banks to take in the area's stunning Christmas markets, sparkling lights, and towering green spruce trees, festive cruises are very popular. Look for itineraries that include Basel, Strasbourg, Rüdesheim am Rhein, and Cologne, all of which have fantastic holiday markets.

Rhine River Cruises for Seven Nights

Seven-night or eight-day cruises frequently depart from Amsterdam (with an overnight stay on board) and travel to Basel via Cologne, Koblenz, the Rhine Gorge, Rudesheim, Mannheim, and Strasbourg. They can also travel the opposite direction, departing from Basel and traveling from Amsterdam. These excursions leave the Rhine to explore the Moselle and Main rivers' highlights. Depending on the route, some boarding and disembarkation stations may be in Luxembourg, Amsterdam, Trier, Bernkastel-Kues, Cochem, Koblenz (through the Moselle), Mainz, Rudesheim, or Cologne.

Others begin or end in Frankfurt or journey from Amsterdam to Avignon via the Rhine and Rhone rivers, stopping in the Netherlands, Germany, and France along the way.

14-night or longer Rhine River Cruises

If you have more time, you may go from Amsterdam to Budapest through Cologne,

Rudesheim, and Nuremberg on a 14-night river cruise. You'll also stop in Passau and other German cities along the way, as well as Budapest, Bratislava, Melk, and Vienna in Austria.

Three-week North Sea to Black Sea voyages from Amsterdam to Bucharest are among the longer alternatives. These cross Germany, Austria, Slovakia, Hungary, Slovenia, Serbia, and Bulgaria and run along the Main, Danube, and Rhine rivers.

Cruise Types and Companies

- Luxury River Cruises:

The height of luxury and style may be found on a river cruise down the Rhine. Small to midsize ships with roomy staterooms—often with balconies— are popular on these cruises.

Expect fine cuisine, high-end wines and spirits, individualized service, and tastefully decorated lounges and public areas as amenities. Guided shore excursions, wellness programs, and entertainment options are common features of luxury cruises.

Tauck River Cruises, Uniworld Boutique River Cruise Collection, and Crystal River Cruises are a few examples.

- <u>Family-Friendly River Cruises:</u>

Families with children of all ages are catered to on family-friendly River Rhine cruises. These cruises are a great option for multigenerational travel since they offer family-friendly activities and amenities.

Amenities: Look for family-friendly cabins or suites, kid's clubs, kid-friendly excursions, and kid- and teen-friendly entertainment alternatives. On some cruises, young travelers can participate in educational activities.

There are several examples, including AmaWaterways Family River Cruises, Viking River Cruises (Viking Longships provide family accommodations), and Adventures by Disney River Cruises.

- Adventure and active cruises:

Cruises on the Rhine that emphasize adventure and physical activity are intended for tourists looking for more strenuous activities. These cruises frequently include outdoor activities like biking, hiking, and other sports.

Amenities: You can anticipate guided bicycling tours along the riverbanks, hikes through picturesque areas, and kayaking and paddling choices. Even guides with plenty of experience are included on some trips.

Examples include Amadeus Active River Cruises, Backroads River Cruises, and A-ROSA's E-Motion Ships (a cruise line featuring electric bikes).

- Educational and cultural cruises

The history, art, and culture of the regions along the Rhine are explored in-depth on cultural and educational cruises. These cruises frequently include guest lecturers and activities with a theme.

Amenities: Look for onboard specialists who offer lectures and workshops about the history and culture of the Rhine. Excursions could include guided tours of historical places, art galleries, and museums.

Avalon Waterways' "Discovery Cruises," Viking River Cruises' "Culture Curriculum," and Grand

Circle Cruise Line's "Local Life" excursions are a few examples.

- Solo Traveler-Friendly Cruises:

Cruises that are especially designed for solo travelers provide a range of amenities. These cruises frequently provide amenities and rates that are intended to make traveling alone more convenient and enjoyable.

Amenities: Search for single-occupancy accommodations that don't charge a large solo premium. There are frequently social events and meal options that encourage lone travelers to interact with other passengers.

Examples include the "Solo Traveler Savings" offered by Uniworld Boutique River Cruise Collection, the "Solo Traveler Program" offered by AmaWaterways, and Riviera Travel's solo river cruises.

- <u>Gate 1 Travel offers the most affordable Rhine River cruises.</u>

The cost of a Rhine River cruise can be unexpected for travelers on a tight budget who are used to finding discounts on ocean-going cruise lines. Gate 1 Travel manages to be one of the top Rhine River cruises for people managing their budget because it costs roughly $1,000 less than the closest rival.

One factor contributing to the cheaper Gate 1 rates is the fact that only dinnertime is when beer, wine, and soda are offered free of charge. Additionally, there are fewer options for dining on ships, both in terms of menus and locations. Step-out balconies are also absent from the Gate 1 ships, though to be fair, many other river cruise companies also lack them. Wi-Fi, an excursion in each port, and admission fees are all included in your price.

Additionally, there are more onboard activities on Gate 1 trips than on a traditional river cruise, including bingo, trivia, and early-morning workout sessions.

- <u>Emerald Cruises is a fantastic choice for Young Travellers</u>

looking for the best Rhine River trip for younger passengers. Modern ships of the more affordable branch of the all-inclusive Scenic line, owned by Australia, frequently draw a significantly younger clientele.

EmeraldACTIVE choices are available on excursions on Emerald's Rhine sailings, including guided bike tours around places like the charming hamlet of Breisach or to the windmills outside of Amsterdam. Another alternative is a trek from Mount Konigstuhl to Heidelberg.

The glass-enclosed swimming pool that transforms into a movie theater at night (complete with popcorn) is a noteworthy feature of the ships. Additionally, Emerald Cruises employs activity coordinators to plan daytime and nighttime activities as well as shore excursions.

- The best Rhine River cruise line for senior citizens is Viking River Cruises

Viking River Cruises is a well-liked brand among senior travelers because of its culturally diverse itineraries. As opposed to merely skimming the surface of a location, Viking lays a strong emphasis on designing trips that offer a real perspective. The service also offers solutions for everyone and is very sensitive of any mobility concerns its patrons may have.

To help visitors determine their level of comfort, Viking River's shore excursions are categorized as simple, moderate, or challenging. The cruise director will go into great detail about what to expect, such as whether there will be any steps or cobblestone streets involved and how much time will be spent walking, during the daily port talk, which summarizes the activities for the following day.

- Best AmaWaterways Rhine River Cruise for Food Lovers

If you're a foodie or wine enthusiast, AmaWaterways is the ideal option for traveling the Rhine River. The Chaine des Rotisseurs is a prominent worldwide culinary society, and all of AmaWaterways' European ships are members. Additionally enhancing the gourmet credentials is the line's cozy Chef's Table restaurant, where all passengers receive a complimentary meal just once while on board.

AmaWaterways offers specialized wine excursions on the Rhine that come with improved gastronomic experiences as part of the price. A knowledgeable wine host leads aboard tastings and conversations during these sailings and goes along on excursions to nearby wineries and vineyards.

Travel documents that are necessary

If you are a citizen of the United States, you must have a current passport in order to travel to and from the Netherlands (Holland), France, Germany, and Switzerland. It must have at least 2 blank pages left and be valid for six months beyond the length of your anticipated stay. If you're renewing an old passport or applying for a new one, give yourself enough time for your application to be processed. -For more information, go to the U.S. Department of State.

Note: For stays of up to 90 days within each 180-day period, visas are not required for travel to Switzerland, France, Germany, and the Netherlands (Holland).

Guests who are 17 years of age or younger who are traveling with a single parent might need to present supplementary identification.

Please contact the consulates or embassies of Switzerland, France, Germany, and The Netherlands (Holland) for information on documentation requirements if you are not a citizen of the United States.

CHAPTER SIX

RHINE RIVER WATER LEVELS: BEFORE YOU CRUISE

One of the most recognizable rivers in all of Europe is the Rhine. But like all rivers, the Rhine River is subject to the whims of the seasons and the vagaries of the weather. If you plan to take a cruise on the Rhine, it's vital to be aware of water levels. Over the years, cruise lines have learned how to manage those effects, and disruptions aren't very frequent.

What Influences Changes in Rhine Water Levels?

Seasonal weather trends affect the Rhine River's water levels. Vessels cannot pass through locks or fit under bridges when the river is too high. Heavy rainfall in the spring and early summer as well as snowmelt in the Alps are typically to blame for high water levels.

On the other hand, the Rhine river's water level decreases as a result of droughts and extremely hot weather, both of which have been increasingly frequent in Western Europe during the past three decades. Ships cannot navigate the Rhine when the water level is severely low because they risk running aground.

In general, low water levels on the Rhine are more frequent than high ones. The warmest and driest season of the year, from late July through August, and perhaps beyond, is when this is most likely to occur. For instance, Europe saw one of its driest years and summers on record in 2022. Germany's drought that year had a significant influence on Rhine water levels, disrupting shipping and even forcing some cruises to take other routes across land in some locations.

Which Section of the Rhine Is Most Affected by the Level of the Water?

The Middle Rhine Valley, a picturesque area recognized by UNESCO, is where the Rhine is shallowest. At Kaub, a water level measurement station continuously keeps track of the river's water level. This makes this section of the Rhine more vulnerable to changes in water levels.

When the Rhine's water levels are low, can cruises still depart?

Due to their extremely shallow drafts, river cruise ships are typically able to travel even during dry spells or low water levels. In reality, even when big commercial barges must stop, river ships can frequently keep cruising the Rhine. On Rhine river cruises, all river cruise companies keep an eye on the water levels and have strategies in place to alter routes as necessary.

What Takes Place During Too Extreme Rhine Water Levels?

Extreme Rhine water levels can be managed by river cruise lines in a variety of methods. If the river is impassable, coach buses may occasionally travel over land to the destinations and to the excursions at each port. However, you must keep in mind that traveling by bus will take more time than by other means of transportation because the distances between ports on the road are typically greater than those on the river. The line may arrange hotel overnight stays en route if these distances grow too great.

Larger lines, like Viking, have a large fleet of ships operating on the Rhine, so guests may travel part of the way on one ship, then be transferred, along with their luggage, to the exact same stateroom on another ship for the remainder of their journey.

The worst-case scenario is that Rhine water levels force the cancellation of your cruise, but this rarely happens. In those circumstances, cruise lines typically get in touch with passengers to explain the situation and frequently provide the chance to rebook the cruise at no additional cost. Communication might be delayed close to the departure date due to the unpredictability and rapid changes in water levels, though.

How Can I Check the Rhine's Water Levels?

If you have a reservation for an upcoming Rhine river trip, the trip Critic forums have a helpful topic that tracks and updates on Rhine water levels. Since it is frequently updated with data and intelligence, bookmark it so that you always have it handy. Other helpful websites that provide information on the Rhine River's water levels by month of the year are Rhine Forecast.

CHAPTER SEVEN

CUISINE IN RHINE RIVER CRUISE

- <u>German treats</u>

Start your culinary journey with Sauerbraten, a traditional German dish. This pot roast is slow-cooked to exquisite perfection and served with a thick, sweet-sour sauce after being marinated in a blend of vinegar and wine. For the complete experience, serve it with potato dumplings and red cabbage.

In some areas, the regional Sauerbraten dish known as Rheinischer Sauerbraten is prepared with horse flesh. It's a local specialty, so don't be shocked if you see it on the menu.

- Flammkuchen

Flammkuchen is a deliciously thin, crispy pizza-like meal that may be found in the Alsace area of France. It's a savory delight topped with cream, onions, and bacon that goes great with a bottle of local Riesling wine.

- Choucroute Garnie

Choucroute Garnie, a robust dish of sauerkraut cooked with a variety of sausages and pig and frequently served with mustard and potatoes, is another delicacy from Alsace.

- Italian Fondue

Don't miss the chance to savor Swiss cheese fondue as you get closer to Switzerland. You dip pieces of bread into the creamy richness of the melted cheese, which is typically a Gruyère and

Emmental blend, which is provided in a communal pot. It's a tasty and enjoyable dining experience.

- <u>Dutch Specialties</u>

Try some pickled herring in the Netherlands. Although it may sound strange, the thing is a popular local treat. It's a special delight you won't find anywhere else, served with pickles and onions.

- <u>Wine sampling</u>

Additionally, the Rhine Valley is well known for its winemaking. Take a break from the filling meals and stroll among the riverside vineyards. Pinot Noir, Riesling, and Gewürztraminer are just a few of the superb wines you may drink while taking in the breathtaking scenery.

- <u>Enticing treats</u>

Without dessert, no gastronomic adventure is complete. Try a Dutch stroopwafel, a tiny waffle biscuit filled with sweet syrup, or the fabled Black

Forest Cake (Schwarzwälder Kirschtorte) from the German Black Forest.

- <u>River cruise dining</u>

Consider taking a river cruise to maximize your Rhine gastronomic experience. While you enjoy the scenic grandeur of the Rhine, many cruise ships offer gourmet dining experiences with regional delicacies and wine pairings.

CHAPTER EIGHT

ON BOARD ACTIVITIES ON RHINE RIVER

You can enjoy health activities on board a Rhine River cruise that will help you relax, recharge, and make the most of your trip in addition to being treated to beautiful scenery and lovely villages. On your Rhine River trip, you can look forward to the following wellness activities:

Wellness activity

Yoga on the Deck: To begin your day, practice yoga in the early morning hours while listening to the tranquil sounds of the river from the open deck. It's the ideal method to stimulate your senses and reconnect with the natural world.

Spa and massage services are typically available on river cruise ships. Enjoy a soothing massage or facial while admiring the beautiful surroundings. The calm is only enhanced by the ship's soft swing.

Fitness sessions

Participate in onboard fitness sessions to stay active while on your vacation. You can select a class based on your level of fitness and interests, ranging from stretching and aerobics to core exercises.

Enjoy excellent, wholesome meals made by the onboard chefs who place a priority on using local, fresh products. Numerous cruise lines have specialty menus with wholesome selections to accommodate a variety of dietary needs.

Join guided meditation classes to help you connect with the present and achieve inner peace through meditation and mindfulness. It's the perfect location for practicing mindfulness because of the river's regular flow and the serene surroundings.

Wellness Lectures: Through interesting onboard lectures, learn about wellness, diet, and mindfulness. Experts frequently offer useful advice on how to lead a healthy lifestyle while traveling.

Pool and Jacuzzi: Heated pools and Jacuzzis are common on river cruise ships. After a long day of sightseeing, relax your muscles with a relaxing swim. During clear nights, take advantage of the Rhine's low level of light pollution by stargazing. The deck is a great place to enjoy the night's silence and connect with the sky while stargazing.

Shops onboard: Some cruise ships contain shops that sell wellness items like teas, bath salts, and essential oils. These are wonderful keepsakes and might improve your leisure time.

Finding a quiet area on the deck to relax in while reading a book, drinking herbal tea, or conversing in silence with other passengers can occasionally be the ideal wellness exercise.

Games on the deck

A Rhine River cruise offers a wonderful balance of excitement and leisure. There are plenty of entertaining games and activities on board to keep you occupied as you take in the breathtaking views. On your Rhine River trip, you can have fun playing the following games on the deck:

- Chess or checkers on the deck: Huge chess and checker sets are frequently offered.

While taking in the gorgeous river views, challenge your fellow passengers to a friendly game and use your strategic thinking.

- Shuffleboard is a traditional cruise game that is great for friendly rivalry. Aim for the highest score possible as you push the discs along the deck's flat surface.
- Bocce Ball: Popular on many river cruises, bocce ball is a fun and friendly activity. Roll the weighted balls across the deck while having fun and striving for accuracy.
- Ping-pong: On the deck of certain ships, there are ping-pong tables. Play entertaining matches to make your games even more memorable against the picturesque setting.

Join the onboard trivia and quiz nights to test your general knowledge. It's more than simply a game; it's an opportunity to socialize with other travelers and perhaps win some amazing prizes.

Bring your preferred card or board games, and join your friends and fellow travelers for a casual game night on the deck.

- Walking and bicycling: Some cruises provide escorted walking or bicycling excursions, and you can even go on a "scavenger hunt" through the charming Rhine towns.
- Deck Parties: A lot of Rhine River cruises throw dancing and live music-filled deck parties. It's a great way to unwind, mingle, and enjoy yourself in the great outdoors.
- Join trivia contests and quizzes being hosted on the deck. It's enjoyable and a wonderful

chance to discover valuable information about the areas you're traveling through.

- Wine and Beer Tasting: Although not a traditional game, onboard wine and beer tastings are a pleasant way to engage in games of the taste, particularly as you try local delicacies while taking in the vistas of the river.

Culture and Craft Workshops

- Cooking demonstrations: Participate in engaging cooking demonstrations guided by expert chefs to learn about regional culinary customs. Learn the techniques to make delicious regional foods so you can make them at home.
- Craft workshops: Practice your skills with local crafts. These classes provide you the opportunity to immerse yourself in the regional craft traditions by teaching you how

to make your own traditional trinkets and wine cork crafts.

- Onboard art sessions can help you to discover your creative side. These classes provide the opportunity for painters of all skill levels to depict the visual grandeur of the Rhine in their own works of art.

- Sharpen your photographic skills with training from industry professionals. Like a pro, capture the breathtaking scenery, charming towns, and important historical sites.

- Learn the fundamentals of the language and dazzle the locals with your improved language abilities. These lectures encourage cultural ties while also enhancing your trip experience.

- Daily talks

In-depth discussions on each destination will take you deep within it. Learn about the towns and cities along the Rhine's history, geography, and undiscovered attractions.

- Local customs: Learn about the distinctive festivals, traditions, and customs of the areas you are visiting. Become more familiar with the history and culture of each port.

- Historical Narratives: Learn about the region of the Rhine's history. Find out about the legendary characters, castles, and forts that have changed the landscape over time.

- Learn about the local flora and animals and the conservation efforts being made along the Rhine as you travel through magnificent surroundings.

- Cultural events: Attend live music and dance events that highlight the Rhine region's rich artistic history.

Your Rhine River cruise is made deeper and richer by these cultural seminars and lectures. They let you to take in the lively culture, crafts, and tales of the destinations you travel to in addition to their stunning natural beauty. These activities provide a wonderful opportunity to discover and value the Rhine's multifarious charm, whether you're eager to become a gourmet connoisseur, a creative craftsman, a budding linguist, or simply a better knowledgeable visitor

Guest Acts

- Top-tier comedians will have you in stitches with their comedy and wit, so get ready to laugh out loud. It's a great way to unwind and take in some fun entertainment.

- Dancers: Dance performances that span from traditional ballet to contemporary interpretations will captivate you. These performances' beauty and elegance give your journey a dash of creative brilliance.

- Singers: Skillful singers enter the stage to wow you with their lovely voices. These vocalists produce a lovely environment that reflects the essence of the Rhine while performing everything from opera arias to contemporary pop songs.

- Speakers: Let informative lectures from special guests broaden your thinking. They provide you with a deeper understanding of the locations you are traveling to by covering a variety of subjects, such as history, culture, and current events.

- Special Occasions:

Stargazing: On evenings with clear skies, go to the upper deck for a surreal experience. The Rhine River offers a superb backdrop for learning about the constellations and other celestial wonders because there is less light pollution there.

- Film Showings: Take in open-air movie showings beneath a starry sky. It's a special and comfortable way to watch a vintage film or a documentary while taking in the serene beauty of the river.

- Experience themed nights at events like vintage dance parties, masquerade balls, or cultural exhibitions. You can immerse yourself in a variety of the culture and entertainment of the area at these events.

- Concerts: Some cruises provide live musical performances, with outstanding artists playing a variety of musical genres to suit a variety of preferences.

- Explore the worlds of wine and gastronomy at events including pairings and exclusive samples. As you travel through wine areas along the Rhine, sample regional wines and fine cuisine.
- Art Exhibitions: View the creations of regional artists in onboard exhibitions. It's a special chance to take in the creativity and talent of the area.
- Interactive Workshops: Attend workshops that allow you to interact directly with regional customs, such as classes in traditional craft-making and cuisine as well as music and dance.
- Live Music

Our skilled onboard musician and singer will serenade you with a wide variety of music throughout your journey. Their performances provide the ideal atmosphere for every stage of your journey, including anything from calming melodies during supper to energetic tunes for dancing. You'll discover that live music adds a special touch to your evenings, whether it be the soothing guitar strumming or the lyrical vocalist.

- Silent Clubs:

We hold silent discos on board for a special and immersive experience. You can listen to the music of your choice with wireless headphones when participating in this contemporary take on the classic dance party. The music may be changed between channels to suit your mood, and you can dance the night away on the upper deck or in a designated location. The idea of a silent disco not only guarantees a private and customized experience but also allows you to dance under the stars without disturbing the peaceful Rhine River surroundings.

Live music and silent discos together provide a lively and adaptable evening entertainment program that appeals to a variety of preferences. Our onboard music and disco experiences are made to make your nights on the Rhine River cruise as special as the days, whether you choose to sway to relaxing melodies, dance to your favorite tunes, or enjoy a bit of both.

Game shows and quizzes

Quizzes and game shows are entertaining and interactive, utilizing cutting-edge technology to heighten the appeal. You can test your knowledge and compete with other passengers on a variety of subjects, ranging from geography to history and everything in between.

Digital devices:

You can have access to digital devices so that you can take part in these fun and mentally challenging

97

games. You can respond to questions, work out riddles, and communicate with the quiz or game show host in real time using these mobile gadgets. Technology keeps the competition vibrant and fair by providing quick feedback in addition to an element of excitement.

Different Topics:

Our quizzes and game shows ask questions on a variety of subjects. There is something for everyone, regardless of your interest in history, geographic prowess, or general knowledge problems. You'll find that participating in these activities is a great way to acquire new information while having fun.

Awards and Appreciation:

Try your brains out while competing for prizes. Our game shows and quizzes give you the chance to shine and earn well-deserved recognition, whether it's a modest gift of praise or the satisfaction of showing your knowledge.

While floating the scenic Rhine River, these engaging interactive game shows and quizzes are a great way to relax and stimulate your mind. It's not just about relaxation; it's also about having a good time, discovering new things, and engaging in intriguing conversation with other passengers. So, get ready to showcase your skills and revel in the excitement of competition while on your trip!

COMMUNICATION AND LANGUAGE WITH THE LOCALS

Here are some important things to keep in mind when communicating with locals while on your Rhine River cruise:

- <u>Language Variation:</u>
Several nations, including Germany, France, the Netherlands, Switzerland, and Belgium, are bordered by the Rhine River. These nations each have a unique official tongue or dialect. Despite the fact that English is a common language in tourist regions and on cruises, it's always a good idea to acquire a few fundamental words and phrases in the local tongue, such "hello," "please," and "thank you." This small gesture can greatly improve your contacts with locals and is frequently appreciated by them.

- English language ability

Particularly in bigger cities and popular tourist locations along the Rhine, English is widely spoken. Many residents, especially those working in the service sector, have a strong grasp of English. However, you might run into fewer English speakers in more rural and small-town settings. A translation app or phrasebook might be quite helpful in such circumstances.

- Guided Tours:

You will benefit from having English-speaking tour guides who are knowledgeable about the regional history and culture during guided tours and shore excursions. They are essential in overcoming the language barrier and giving you insightful information about the places you travel.

- Regional Accents:

Local dialects may vary from standard German in some areas, particularly in Germany. Although it can be difficult to understand these languages, locals are used to communicating with tourists and will frequently convert to standard German or English if necessary.

- Observe regional customs:

Respecting local norms and traditions is crucial while conversing with locals. The ability to communicate effectively across language obstacles can be facilitated by politeness and a nice approach. When expressing kindness, a grin and a respectful nod can go a far way.

- Tools & Apps for Translation:

To facilitate communication, keep a pocket dictionary or a translation software with you. When you need to ask inquiries or explain specific information but your English is poor, these tools can be extremely helpful.

- <u>Body Language</u>

Body language can serve as a universal language when words would be inadequate. You can convey your message more effectively by using gestures, pointing, and nonverbal cues.

Interacting with residents along the Rhine River may be a fun and educational experience. Despite any linguistic barriers, most people are accustomed to engaging with foreign tourists and are frequently ready to help. Your travel experience will be considerably improved if you are open-minded, courteous, and willing to put forth the effort to acquire a few local words and phrases. This will also encourage pleasant encounters with the kind people you'll come across along the road.

GREAT PHOTOGRAPHY TIPS

- Get comfortable holding your camera.

Even while it might seem simple, many amateur photographers handle their cameras incorrectly, which results in camera shake and poor pictures. The ideal approach to eliminate camera shake is, of course, to use a tripod, but since you won't be using one unless you're shooting in low light, it's crucial to hold your camera securely to prevent unneeded movement.

Even if you'll eventually find your own preferred method of holding the camera, you should always do so. To support the weight of the camera, position your left hand behind the lens while holding the right side of the camera in your right hand.

The camera will be easier for you to hold motionless the closer you keep it to your body. If you need more stability, you can stoop down or lean against a wall, but if there is nothing to lean against, taking a broader stance can also be beneficial.

- Start your RAW capture.

While RAW is a file format similar to JPEG, it does not compress the image data; instead, it preserves all of it. In addition to getting photographs of superior quality when you shoot in RAW, you'll also have much more control over the editing process. For instance, you'll be able to alter things like color temperature, white balance, and contrast, as well as fix issues like overexposure or underexposure.

The files require greater storage space when shot in RAW, which is a drawback. Additionally, RAW images necessitate post-processing, necessitating the purchase of photo editing software.

But ultimately, if you have the time and room, shooting in RAW can drastically improve the quality of your photographs. For thorough instructions on how to convert from jpeg to RAW, consult the manual that came with your camera.

- The exposure triangle to your advantage

The three most crucial components of exposure— ISO, aperture, and shutter speed—are simply referred to as the exposure triangle, despite the fact that it may initially look a bit intimidating. To take sharp, well-lit images when using manual mode, you must be able to balance all three of these factors.

- ISO: ISO regulates the camera's light sensitivity. The camera will be less sensitive to light when the ISO is set low, and more sensitive to light when the ISO is set high. When photographing in low light conditions, such as inside or at night, a higher ISO of 400 to 800 or more may be required. An ISO setting of 100 to 200 is typically ideal.

The opening in your lens known as the aperture determines how much light enters the camera's sensor. More light enters through a wider aperture (represented by a lower f-number), whereas less light enters through a narrow aperture (shown by a higher f-number). When you want to isolate your subject, a wide aperture works well. However, when you want the entire scene to be in focus, as in group photographs, you must choose a tight aperture.

- Best for portraiture is a wide aperture.

The easiest technique to make your subject the center of the photograph while taking portraits, whether of people or animals, is to utilize a larger aperture. This will eliminate any background distractions while keeping your subject sharp.

- For landscapes, a narrow aperture is ideal.

A distinct strategy is needed for landscape photography because the foreground rocks and the distance mountains all need to be sharply in focus. So, choose a narrow aperture rather than a wide one whenever you're shooting a situation where you want everything to be sharp.

According to what your lens permits, aim for f/22 or higher since a greater f/number indicates a narrower aperture. Once more, using Aperture Priority Mode (Av or A) will let you experiment with various apertures without having to constantly change the shutter speed. For extra advice, refer to our depth of field beginner's guide.

- Shutter speed: When taking a photo, shutter speed determines how long the shutter is open. More light reaches the camera's sensor the longer the shutter is open. While a slower shutter speed will cause motion to be blurred, a faster shutter speed is better for freezing action. Visit our blog to learn more about understanding shutter speeds.

- Use the modes Aperture Priority and Shutter Priority. Aperture Priority Mode (A or Av) and Shutter Priority Mode (S or Tv) are two extremely helpful choices that are available on most cameras and will give you more control without being unduly confusing if you want to step out of automatic mode but don't feel confident enough to switch to manual just yet.

You can choose the aperture you want to use in Aperture Priority Mode, and the camera will then change the shutter speed to match. Therefore, you may choose a wide aperture and let the camera choose the optimal shutter speed if you're shooting a portrait and want the background to be blurry.

In shutter priority mode, you choose the desired shutter speed, and the camera automatically chooses the appropriate aperture. So, for instance, if you want to capture your puppy running toward you clearly, you can choose a quick shutter speed and let the camera decide on the aperture.

- Don't be reluctant to increase ISO

Although it's true that utilizing higher ISO might result in lower image quality, there is a time and place for everything. Many photographers try to avoid ever shooting in high ISO because they are scared it would result in grainy-looking photos or "noise."

If motion blur prevents you from lowering your shutter speed and using a tripod isn't an option, it's preferable to take a sharp photo with some noise rather than none at all because you can eliminate most of the noise in post-processing. Additionally, recent advancements in camera technology have made it feasible to take stunning photos even at ISO 1600, 3200, or 6400.

- Use a wider aperture whenever you can to reduce noise when shooting at higher ISOs. Making light regions darker in post-processing won't increase noise, but making dark areas lighter unquestionably will, thus slightly overexposing your image can also help.

- Make it a practice to check your ISO before you take a picture.

It can be really upsetting to learn that you unintentionally captured a whole collection of ISO 800 shots on a sunny day, especially if you were trying to capture a moment in time that can never be replicated, like a birthday or anniversary.

Though it's a simple error to make, develop the practice of verifying and resetting your ISO settings before you begin shooting anything to prevent this unpleasant surprise. Alternately, establish a routine whereby you reset this each time you're about to put your camera back in its bag.

- Use caution when using the camera's flash.

If you're not careful, using the built-in flash of your camera at night or in dim lighting might result in unflattering outcomes like red eyes and sharp shadows. In general, using the on-camera light and running the risk of completely spoiling the photograph is preferable to raising the ISO and getting noisier pictures.

- When there isn't enough light, though, you will occasionally be forced to utilize the built-in flash if you don't have any off-camera lighting. There are a few things you may do if you find yourself in this circumstance and don't want to miss the shot. First, locate the flash settings in the menu of your camera, then minimize brightness as much as possible.

Second, you can try covering the flash with anything to attempt and diffuse the light. The light can be diffused and softened, for instance, by covering the flash with paper or opaque scotch tape. Alternately, you might hold a piece of white cardboard at an angle in front of the ceiling to reflect the light.

- White balance adjustment techniques

You may capture colors more precisely by using white balance. If you don't alter the white balance, the colors in your photographs may take on a faint blue, orange, or green hue or "temperature," as different sources of light have distinct properties.

It is possible to correct white balance in post-processing, but it can get laborious if you have hundreds of photographs that require little modifications. It is therefore preferable to get this setting correct in the camera. Your camera likely has a number of default white balance settings, including Automatic White Balance, Daylight, Cloudy, Flash, Shade, Fluorescent, and Tungsten.

If you're unsure which of them is which because each of them is represented by a different icon, see your camera's manual. Although automatic white balance can be useful in some circumstances, it's usually preferable to adjust the setting to the sort of lighting you're working with.

- Modify your perception.

Experimenting with perspective is the best method to boost your photographic creativity. When viewed from a different angle, the same sight can frequently appear very differently, and photographing a subject from above or below might alter the overall mood of the image.

Of course, not every viewpoint will work for every shot, but if you don't try different things, you'll never find out what does and doesn't. You can try getting on their level and looking at the world through their eyes while shooting animals or kids. Why not use a bench to your advantage when taking a portrait and shooting your subject from above?

- Recognize the law of thirds.

The notion behind the rule of thirds is that visuals tend to be more fascinating and well-balanced when they aren't in the center. Consider overlaying your photographs with a grid that consists of two vertical and two horizontal lines that divide each image into nine equal portions.

Instead of placing your subject or the crucial components of a scene in the center of the photograph, you would do so in accordance with the rule of thirds by placing them along one of the four lines or at the intersections of the lines. If you're still learning how to compose your photos, some cameras even include a grid setting you can activate.

Of course, photography is all about creativity and individual expression, so you could occasionally decide to deviate from this rule and place the main subjects of your image somewhere else. This is completely OK, but it's crucial that you grasp it and get into the habit of deliberately considering the points of interest and where you want to place them before you start breaking this guideline. Find out more about our collection of compositional strategies for better photography.

- Always maintain eye focus.

It is crucial that you capture a nice, sharp image when taking portraits because you will be concentrating on a very small area. Particularly in close-ups and headshots, the eyes are a crucial facial feature that are frequently the first thing viewers notice.

In light of this, your main point of focus should be your subject's eyes. Select one focus point and point it at one of the eyes to get both eyes nice and sharp. Once the first eye is sharp, move the camera just a little bit while keeping the shutter button halfway down to recompose the image to include the second eye.

- Take note of the background

In general, the background should be as uncluttered and uncomplicated as possible to avoid detracting from the photograph's main subject. Because you don't want viewers to become more interested in the colorful building or church tower in the background than your model, muted colors and simple patterns frequently work well.

Moving your subject or changing your angle can often fix a distracting background, but if that doesn't work, you might be able to blur it by using a wider aperture and getting as close to your subject as you can. However, whenever you can, try to avoid adding any color to the background, especially if your subject is off to the side of the frame and the background is clearly visible. Check out our guide to minimalist photography for more advice.

- Purchase a tripod

If you want to produce sharp photographs in low light without boosting the ISO too much, a tripod is an essential device. It will also allow you to experiment with long exposure photography, where you leave the shutter open for seconds or even minutes at a time, which can provide for some stunning effects when capturing things like cityscapes or rivers and waterfalls.

When purchasing your first tripod, there are a few things to consider such as weight, stability and height. Weight is crucial because you'll be carrying the tripod about with you and don't want anything too heavy, but it also needs to be solid enough to handle your camera and the lenses you want to use. You can hear more about what we propose for improving your photography gear with our blog.

- Be discerning

It's critical to understand that every photographer, regardless of experience or talent, takes some subpar pictures. They don't bore you with ten images of a practically identical situation, which is why their portfolios are so amazing; instead, they only show you their best work.

Therefore, aim to choose just a handful of excellent photographs from each shoot if you want your work to stand out when you share it on Facebook, Instagram, or other photo-sharing websites. Even if you took hundreds of images at your friend's birthday party or your son's football game, hiding the five or ten truly outstanding ones from view will prevent you from seeing them.

- Take note of your errors.

It can be unpleasant to take images that are overexposed, blurry, or poorly composed, but instead of letting them demotivate you, utilize them as a teaching tool. The next time you take a terrible picture, resist the urge to delete it right away. Instead, take some time to analyze the picture to determine what went wrong and how you could make it better.

The majority of the time, there will be a straightforward fix, such as experimenting with a different composition or utilizing a higher shutter speed, but if you encounter any persistent issues, you'll have the opportunity to research particular facets of photography and improve your weaker areas.

- Shoot in the early morning and evening

Lighting can make or break a photo, and the early morning and evening are commonly believed to be the ideal times of day for capturing photos. In photography, the hour soon after the sun rises or before it sets is dubbed the "golden hour," since the sun is lower in the sky and the light is softer and warmer. Whether you're photographing landscapes, portraits or still life, employing the early morning or evening light may give your images a tranquil atmosphere with its warm glow and the lengthy shadows it forms. Of course, the golden hour is not the only time you can obtain beautiful outdoor shots, but it does make it simpler.

- Invest in some nice photo editing software

Once you start shooting in RAW, post processing will become a requirement rather than an afterthought, therefore you'll need to invest in some photo editing software that will allow you to conduct basic editing jobs such as cropping, altering exposure, white balance and contrast, erasing blemishes and more.

Most professional photographers use applications like Adobe Photoshop or Lightroom, but if you want something a little less pricey to start with you can try Photoshop Elements, Picasa or Paint Shop Pro.

Capturing Memories on the River Rhine Cruise

_____
_____
_____
_____
_____
_____
_____
_____
_____
_____
_____
_____
_____
_____
_____
_____
_____
_____
_____
_____
_____
_____
_____
_____
_____
_____

Made in the USA
Las Vegas, NV
07 January 2024

84018770R00075